GROUND OF ALL BEING:
The Prayer of Jesus in Color

John Philip Newell

Photographs by Claudia Tammen

GROUND OF ALL BEING:
The Prayer of Jesus in Color

John Philip Newell

Photographs by Claudia Tammen

© John Philip Newell 2008
Photographs © Claudia Tammen 2008
www.materialmedia.net

ISBN 978-0-9819800-0-3

Cover Photograph by Claudia Tammen

New Beginnings
An Imprint of Material Media
San Antonio, Texas
www.MaterialMedia.Net

Printed in China

Contents

to Rob & Lyn Houk
with gratitude

R.I.P.

My friends at
Christ Church
Cathedral, Houston)
Rosemary deceased.
MfS

PREFACE

This project was conceived in the summer of 2007 at Ghost Ranch in the high desert of New Mexico. My wife Alison, in conversation over lunch one day with the photographer Claudia Tammen, said, "Why don't you and Philip collaborate on a publication?" That was enough to sow the seed. Ground of All Being: The Prayer of Jesus in Color is a collaboration of word and image, of sound and sight. It combines the poetry of the Prayer of Jesus with the landscape photography of Claudia Tammen.

The words we are using are from Casa del Sol, the little retreat house at Ghost Ranch Conference Center. Companions of Casa del Sol describe themselves as "a community of the Living Presence, seeking the oneness of the human soul and the healing of creation." Our version of the Prayer of Jesus, which we sing at the rising and setting of the sun each day, is an attempt to give voice to a new sound of spirituality for today inspired by the ancient teachings of Jesus. It echoes the growing awareness of the earth's oneness. Similarly, Claudia's photographs are born out of this landscape and reflect the desire to hold together spirituality and love of the earth.

But how are we to use this combination of sight and sound? For some it may simply be a bedside or coffee table book, to occasionally remember a landscape that is like a living icon of the divine Presence. For others it will be more like a daily prayer book in which a single phrase and image combined can be meditated upon or in which the whole prayer can be uttered and viewed at one sitting. A journaling section has been added as an appendix to the book to provide space for keeping a journal of response to the phrases and photographs. However the book is used, may it constantly remind us of the Oneness from whom we have come and the one earth to which we belong.

Special thanks to Elizabeth Cauthorn for graciously managing this project, to Jim Baird and Casa del Sol's other Companion Advisors for providing the seed-money to make it possible, to Ghost Ranch Conference Center - the mother of Casa del Sol - to whom all profits from this publication are dedicated, and especially to Claudia Tammen whose landscapes are the inspiration and the beauty of this book.

John Philip Newell
Casa del Sol
October 2008

CASA DEL SOL PRAYER OF JESUS

Ground of all being,
Mother of life,
Father of the universe,
Your name is sacred, beyond speaking.
May we know your presence,
may your longings be our longings
in heart and in action.
May there be food for the human family today
and for the whole earth community.
Forgive us the falseness of what we have done
as we forgive those who are untrue to us.
Do not forsake us in our time of conflict
but lead us into new beginnings.
For the light of life,
the vitality of life,
and the glory of life
are yours now and for ever.
Amen.

Ground of all being,

Mother of life,

Father of the universe,

Your name is sacred, beyond speaking.

May we know your presence,

may your longings be our longings

in heart and in action.

May there be food for the human family today

and for the whole earth community.

Forgive us the falseness of what we have done

as we forgive those who are untrue to us.

Do not forsake us in our time of conflict

but lead us into new beginnings.

For the light of life,

the vitality of life,

and the glory of life

are yours now and for ever.

Amen.

Ground of all being,

Mother of life,
Father of the universe,

Your name is sacred, beyond speaking.

May we know your presence,

may your longings be our longings
in heart and in action.

May there be food for the human family today
and for the whole earth community.

Forgive us the falseness of what we have done
as we forgive those who are untrue to us.

Do not forsake us in our time of conflict
but lead us into new beginnings.

For the light of life,
the vitality of life,

and the glory of life
are yours now and for ever.

Amen.

APPENDIX: Photograph Locations

CASA DEL SOL

Casa del Sol is a retreat house at Ghost Ranch Conference Center in the high desert of New Mexico. It hosts a variety of retreats and spirituality courses, both for individual use and for community building. It is the base of The Companions of Casa del Sol, a network of men and women throughout the country who are committed to being 'a community of the Living Presence, seeking the oneness of the human soul and the healing of creation.'

For more information, please contact:
Carole Landess, the Companion Host of Casa del Sol
casadelsol@ghostranch.org

Author & Photographer

John Philip Newell, Companion Theologian for the
Community of Casa del Sol, lives in Edinburgh with his wife
Alison and their four children. He is a wandering scholar and
the author of many books, including *Listening for the
Heartbeat of God* and *Christ of the Celts*.

www.jphilipnewell.com

Claudia Tammen finds joy in photography both as vocation and
avocation. She lives in Orange County, CA and visits Ghost
Ranch (where she lived and worked for five years) as often as
possible. Her first book of photography, *Ghost Ranch Vistas
& Visions*, was published in 2006.

www.claudiatammen.smugmug.com